The

Thoughts

Of A

Virgin

Explicit on Purpose

Idella Liselle

Scripture quotations taken from the Amplified® Bible, Copyright © 1954, 1958, 1962, 1964, 1965, 1987 by The Lockman Foundation
Used by permission. (**www.Lockman.org**)

Scripture quotations from *THE MESSAGE*. Copyright © by Eugene H. Peterson 1993, 1994, 1995, 1996, 2000, 2001, 2002. Used by permission of NavPress Publishing Group.

Scripture quotations marked "ESV" are taken from The Holy Bible: English Standard Version, copyright 2001, Wheaton: Good News Publishers. Used by permission. All rights reserved.

Scripture quotations marked "KJV" are taken from the Holy Bible, King James Version, Cambridge, 1769.

Scripture quotations taken from the New American Standard Bible® (NASB), Copyright © 1960, 1962, 1963, 1968, 1971, 1972, 1973,1975, 1977, 1995 by The Lockman Foundation Used by permission. www.Lockman.org

Copyright © 2019 All rights reserved

International Standard Book Number 13: 978-1948731041

Publish*her* Publishing

www.publishHer.org
www.idellaliselle.com

DEDICATION

THIS BOOK IS DEDICATED TO:

PEOPLE WHO REALLY LIKE SEX YET ARE WAITING TO EXPERIENCE ITS SPLENDOR AND BACK ARCHING GLORY IN ITS DESIGNED HABITAT.

PEOPLE WHO REALLY, REALLY LIKE SEX AND ARE DOING IT, BUT DESIRE TO DO IT GOD'S WAY AND WILL SOON JOIN THE CLUB AND WAIT TOO.

WE LOVE YOU BOTH

TABLE OF CONTENTS

1
WHY

Why am I writing this book? What made me
Why am I writing this book? What made me
want to expose some of the most intimate
details of my life to total strangers? Simply
because I believe being this transparent is
going to help and or free someone. We live in
a   society   that   is   driven   by   sex.
EVERYTHING seems over-sexualized. We
are heavily inundated with sexual overtones to
the point that even our commercials make it
hard to identify precisely what product or
service is marketed.

Add to it the extreme mentality that often
seems connected with Christians/Church
Folks that goes for all or nothing and we have

an ongoing dilemma. This displays itself in the mixed message of cover oneself up from head to toe or let's give it to the people with clothes so tight that even thoughts are exposed. This is where we find ourselves with weak standards and rigid expectations.

I don't want to present myself as an expert on the subject of sex. I am merely someone who is able to share what I have learned. Unfortunately much was through trial and error. I AM A VIRGIN. I am not a born-again virgin but a real bonafide scientifically defined virgin; one who has never had sex. You read correctly, I have never had oral, vaginal, or anal sex. My transparency refuses to allow for any confusion. Even though I have never had sex, I have had sexual encounters. Yes, I have had an orgasm, quite a few actually.

Though a scientifically defined virgin, I would not qualify for a biblical virgin because I have had sex in my mind too many times to count. For those who may not know, Scripture lets us know that which we have done in our minds, we still have culpability for spiritually.

If this seems a little too much, let me explain. Scripture comes from the aspect of "as a man thinketh, so is he." If you lust after a woman in your mind, you have already entered into the sin of the thing. Don't get it twisted. Our liability spiritually can be quickly be remedied with repentance with no natural side effects if not carried out. Having sex in one mind will never produce a baby or get you an STD. HOWEVER, prolonged and continued thoughts on this subject can get you into a level of bondage. Continued strong mental participation on the subject will guarantee very soon; your thoughts will become actions.

Hence, I am not your typical white as the driven snow virgin. I have some muddy tracks in my wake. I am a very sexual being; I believe GOD made me that way. I believe the enemy also knew this and targeted me at a young age to blur the lines. Early on, I was exposed to sexual activity such as pornography and even masturbation. Pile on molestation from a family friend, and it appeared the enemy had created a cocktail for disaster.

Again, I genuinely believe GOD made me

sexual, but the perversion that I had witnessed and later participated in had disturbingly awakened my love waaaay before time. What should have been an amazing exploratory journey with my husband became something sordid with too many hits and misses along the way.

This is the reason I must share? I have been saved since age of three and in church all my known life, (minus three weeks I stayed out and thought I would never come back, you can read that story in my book "Is Church Killing You? Surviving Ministry") yet I have only heard a few people within the church explicitly talk about sex from the desire to empower and equip the body of CRIST to have **healthy** sex lives. I know sex is good for a couple of reasons:

1. GOD created sex
2. People lose their mind over sex
3. People get into a relationship *just* for sex
4. People won't get out of a relationship just for sex
5. My previous orgasms have produced enough evidence that when I do have sex

through marriage, it is going to be worth the wait (I know every time is not going to be earth-shattering, toe-curling and calling out GOD's name amazing but I am sure greater experiences will be in the majority, because greater is He within me...., lol)

My first point is sex is good because GOD created it. In Genesis, we see a principle in play; everything GOD created had a seed in it which is able to produce more. Naturally and spiritually, sex has a seed that can produce more. Check out this list

Emotional Benefits of Having Sex
- Increases level of commitment
- Boosts self-esteem
- Makes a person feel younger
- Lowers the level of cortisol, a hormone that can trigger fatigue and cravings
- Lowers feelings of insecurity
- Keeps spouses connected emotionally
- Helps to give people a more positive attitude
- Makes a person more calm

- Makes a person less irritable
- Reduces depression
- Relieves stress

Physical Benefits of Having Sex

- Reduces risk of physical illness
- Improves immunity
- Reduces pain by increasing endorphins
- It's a form of exercise (it can help people achieve weight loss since about 200 calories are burned during 30 minutes of active sex
- Less-frequent colds and flu
- Vaginal tissue lubrication
- Lower mortality rates
- Reduced risk of prostate cancer
- Offers pain relief, including pain from migraines and back pain
- Improves posture
- Gives a youthful glow
- Reduces risk of heart disease
- Helps prevent yeast infections
- Lightens menstrual periods and cramps
- Firms stomach and buttocks
- Lowers blood pressure
- Helps people sleep better
- Improves digestion

- Improves sense of smell
- Has a therapeutic effect on the immune system
- Better bladder control
- Healthier teeth
- Increased DHEA makes your skin healthier
  Improves fitness level
- Increases circulation
- Improves memory

Taken from Sheri Stritof, entitled, "Why should you have sex more often,"

What an amazing list! We can easily see its ability to reproduce? It was created to be good and have good results. Yet, why are so many "Christian" messages pushing an agenda as if sex is bad? Sex itself is good; however, the parameters in which we place sex determine if what is produced is good according to GOD's purpose or not.

Do not for one moment, believe that I am a virgin because I am repressed in my sexuality or I don't like sex, quite the contrary. I am a virgin because I fully embrace my sexuality. I finally understand the beauty and power of sex and only want to allow it to flourish in its created habitat, marriage.

My previous proclivities had placed me in chains that had me locked up for years. A sad fact of discovery was the key to my liberty was hidden within me. This discovery wasn't gotten overnight. Some of my revelation required painful introspection and courageous confrontation to gain freedom.

I would love to say that my search led me to the wise counsel of pastors and leaders of the churches where I was connected, but paradoxically it was not. Ironically, many of the leaders were battling the same struggles. They were either in silence or in secret celebration of their plight.

This is the reason why someone HAS to talk about it. Are you aware of how many GOD loving and church-going unmarried Christians are still having sex outside of marriage? Some desire to stop but have no earthly idea how. Many don't understand how to deal with those intense desires. Some in error were told it is wrong even to want sex. Which means the natural desire for sex that leads to procreation, which is connected to why we were created, is sinful. This makes our approach imbalanced and yields less than desirable results.

Hopefully, as I share my concise thoughts, a new conversation will emerge. Again, I am by no means the expert. I love the Scripture that says I know in part and prophecy in part and when the perfect comes, that part which is incomplete will be done away. I don't know everything. None of us do. All of us only have a part. I am writing about the part I know so far, but a time will come when even this part will be replaced by a greater understanding.

Something To Think About

1. What are your thoughts about sex? Do you see it as good?

2. What are convictions do you have about sex outside of marriage?

3. Do you have safe godly places to talk about sex without condemnation?

THE MAIN EVENT HAS BEEN CANCELED

I briefly mentioned that my sexual curiosities were awakened at a very young age. I have come to realize that I admittedly have some freakish tendencies. Though I was saved at 3 and in church all of my life, I was still getting my freak on. My concept of wrong and right wouldn't allow me to go all-in. I felt less convicted about dipping my toes in sexual escapades but quickly saw the water had risen to my hoo-haw in my nether regions.

I tried as much as possible to be discreet. My mother had always stressed to us that our name is something important and deserves to be protected. She believed when your name gets tarnished, everything else follows. Being adept at subterfuge, I attempted to keep all of my activity on the low. As a teenager, I would never sit on the back row. The reputation was well known about the girls who sat in the back row with coats covering them in the hot of the summer. I never sat in the back; however, on the second row, with my jacket covering us, I participated in some not so godly activity with my boyfriend. I only brought out my jacket on cool days. At the age of 15, I was attached to a 19-year old boyfriend. I saw attached because we never really defined our relationship. Before you get all judgy on the age gap, he had just graduated, and I was in the 12th grade.

I was very mature for my age and well respected by peers and adults in my community. However, I was attracted to this bad boy. He exposed to me things sexually that fed my freak and always had me wanting more.

We had progressed from the hand holding to consistent heavy petting. But one night, sitting in my living room with my two younger sisters in another room, he had excited me to the point that I had forgotten all of my many nos. I was ready to have sex. I was like, "let's do it." Anatomically, he was obviously prepared for the action, but he looked up with eyes glazed and said something I was not quite ready for. "We can't." I went blank for a moment and was like, huh?!!. He continued to say, "If we have sex right now, you will end up hating me and hating yourself."

My 15-year old passion was immediately replaced with anger. This niagra had been begging me for weeks to have sex, and now that I wanted to, he was not complying. I can now understand it to be divine intervention. He later forgot that he even said that. Needless to say, the night didn't end well because the main event had been canceled.

I was primed and ready. There was so much expectation riding on it only for it not to turn out the way we expected it. At that time, my moment was about having sex. Yet, what about those other to die for moments that caused us to throw caution to the wind because we thought that was "it." Scripture tells us that we are drawn away by our own desires. I couldn't see it then, but what I desired was not what I ultimately wanted.

Thoughts of a Virgin

I was angry and confused. When we didn't
have sex that night, it made me, for a moment,
question me. Was there something wrong with
me? Why didn't he want me? That thought
wasn't entertained for long because reasoning
reminded me that my boyfriend's arousal was
natural proof of desire. If not for that, it would
have easy to continue to fully and wholly
blame myself.

Have you ever been angry or confused
because something didn't happen the way you
wanted it? Through possible insecurities, you
took on full-on blame and responsibility for a
failure?

Internally, you became the sole reason why
something or someone didn't work. You may
have carried that weighty mindset into other
opportunities and relationships.   Those
thoughts of failure create patterns of self-
distrust. It can breed torment with a constant
question of our value and abilities. We start
thinking something must be wrong with us.
We then get to the point where we don't feel
good enough to achieve something and/or
receive something. This is where we start

operating in self-sabotage.

Mindsets like this cause us to miss the big picture. The way I processed my disappointment made it a personal epic fail. I internalized that event as my failure when it was the direct opposite. In that instance I felt rejected when, in truth, I was being protected.

Rejection makes EVERYTHING personal. Rejection isolates the issue to become all about us. It makes it hard to consider outside factors. Once you have experienced rejection all failure can become a personal issue and disappointment becomes abnormally heavy.

Is the way you process your disappointment too heavy to carry? Does it block you from enjoying current activities and hindering healthy relationships? Is there something that you need to think about again? Did you make it personal when in actuality it was purposeful? My purpose refuses to allow some things to happen. I believe the same goes for you.

I am especially grateful for Romans 8:28,

"ALL things work together for the good of them that love Him and called according to His purpose." I don't have to trip over the times that I missed or messed up. If those times are submitted and repented for, even those things have to somehow work for my good. I am still gaining a working understanding of how it works, but I am convinced that all will ultimately work someway or somehow for our good.

I was challenged by GOD to change my mindset from thinking things happen TO me to the belief things happen FOR me. Even the crazy unexplainable thing will ultimately somehow work for me.

Would that thinking be beneficial to you? How would you process life if you start believing things were happening for you and not to you? Could that change the dynamics of your life? Even if an event canceled, you would no longer feel like you were denied something but saved from something or for something.

Something To Think About

1. What didn't go according to plan in life that caused you to question your value or significance?

2. If relationships were investments, has any of them caused you to go bankrupt? Have you been able to recover your losses?

3. How can you reframe your thoughts to go from "it happened to me" to "it happened for me."?

3
TOTALLY NAKED

Coming out of the shower, I walked passed a mirror and paused. I looked at myself totally naked, and smiled at my reflection. It was a smile that represented freedom for which I had long searched. I had struggled with my image on and off for years. I had equated beauty with flawless skin, good hair, and the bomb shape. It wasn't that I was superficial, just influenced. I see beauty from the inside out. However, my way of seeing beauty didn't fall within the popular opinion. I judged things one way, others judged me another.

This was not an isolated event but was reinforced countless times where I would see the superficial was chosen over the substantial. Don't get me wrong. I understand that there must be a physical attraction. I think that plays a major role for many, myself included. One person commented that I never messed with a mud duck, I think "mud duck" it's a southern idiom for someone not physically attractive. So I get it. However, I have never chosen a person solely for their looks, that was a bonus to the other qualities I saw or imagined. I can understand the struggle because there was this one time, where I toiled with a relationship way too long because of his face and his thighs. There is something about powerful football player thighs. He wasn't chosen because of his thighs, but his looks did keep me connected longer than wisdom dictated. Cute typically gets away with more mess than ugly. Even still, I believe what we have promoted as physical beauty is flawed.

I have never thought of myself as ugly, but until a couple of years ago, a word like gorgeous wouldn't readily roll off my tongue when describing myself.

I had reluctantly assimilated to the mainstream identification of beauty and loss out on what beauty really is, even concerning myself. I had allowed a few sporadic distasteful moments overshadow the many encounters to the contrary.

For instance, one time when I was walking with another young lady upstairs to a church event. She was lighter complexion with long hair and a gentleman extended his hand to assist her up the steps but totally ignored me. That incident totally stole night. To this day, I can't tell you what else happened that night because that instance erased the rest of the evening.

It was those few moments that robbed my confidence and pushed me in a corner when I was created to be center stage. Again it wasn't as if I had a lot of these moments, quite the opposite. Yet, I lingered on the negative and allowed it to create a narrative that placed constant questions on my confidence. Scripture tells us, "don't cast your confidence away for it comes with a reward." My mother always said confidence makes a woman more attractive. My limited understanding of what authentic confidence looked like had me faking it with the best of them.

My confidence's fake bravado came off as unapproachable and at times untouchable. I was determined that I would not be hurt by the opinion of others, so I lived life at a distance. Though I could be surrounded by many, I was enclosed in a heavily guarded space where the key was always in my hand. I was pretty good at ensuring no one was getting in.

I had struggled with low self-esteem on many levels. I was unsure of my purpose, my perspective, and my person. I didn't know what I was called to do, how I was called to do, or who I was called to do it as. One night a pastor shared that when you have low self-esteem, the enemy doesn't even have to bother with you. He explained that our insecurities would talk us out of doing whatever GOD called us to do or being whoever GOD called us to be.

There was an immediate recognition that I had fallen into that category. I began studying identity. I looked to Scripture and read other books to build a stronger foundation. I know I was called to be great, but my pressing thought of not being enough was choking the life out of me and everything else alive connected to me.

Though I was getting closer to GOD, I was still grappling with my image. On one fast (a fast is refraining from any solid foods for spiritual purposes), an Apostle(a title referred to type of minister in Christian faith because of their calling) shared very matter of factly, "While you are on this fast seeking GOD, ask Him to reveal you because it is obvious that you don't know who you are."

Well, alrighty then, I thought. I hung up the phone with tears flowing and asked GOD to show me how He saw me. Not long after that call, I had a vision. GOD had escorted me to a waterfall where a lady was standing with her back towards us. It was like she was where she belonged. She emitted this peace with herself and her surroundings. Her silhouette was shapely, but it was as if that was an afterthought. What stood out was the beauty she radiated. Just looking at her, I felt more beautiful. Her presence was powerful. I wanted to know her, I asked GOD who the lady was, and He responded: "This is how I see you." Once again, the tears started falling from my eyes. In that instance, the broken image of my identity was restored to a perfectly flawed beauty. After the vision ended, I was reminded about a time at the age of 17 when I was a missionary in Mexico. One of the other missionaries shared a vision where she saw me at a waterfall, and I looked so beautiful.

GOD was determined that I would fully get this revelation because the same day, one of my friends called me and said: "earlier today, I saw a vision of you at a waterfall, and you looked so beautiful."

I purposed from that day on to embrace my beauty as GOD defined not man.. It was crazy because that mere mind change produced results. While in stores or at events, people would come up and say, "You are so beautiful."

Because this book is about transparency, I must bear it all. Though I had that profound revelation, there are still times I battle with embracing my beauty. Weight has been one of the consistent struggles. In 2007, I lost over 70 pounds and kept it off for 3 years, but after encountering some very emotional battles and the loss of my mom, I put that weight and more back on. I found it hard to quickly embrace the beauty as I once did. It was because, on some level, I still equated beauty to a size.

But that morning totally naked, I viewed my lumps, dumps and humps as beautiful.

I recalled a time years ago, I was asked if I

would be okay with my husband seeing me totally naked with the lights on. In that season of my life, I quickly replied no. Nakedness presents a greater vulnerability and opportunity for rejection. It was complete and utter exposure. I felt the need to cover up. Do you know the need to cover-up was introduced as a result of malfunction?

Adam and Eve were both naked until sin happened. A malfunction occurred to the plan, and then entered the cover-up. Church, if operating in dysfunction, can become a breeding ground for the cover up. When we foster environments that demand absolute perfection, it tends to create the need for a deceptive façade. No one is willing to bare it all in fear of rejection.

I once wounded my hand. It was an unsightly gash, so I continued to cover it up. The result was an infection. I was advised that I needed to take off the cover so it can get better. Is there something in your life that you feel is unsightly but covering it up has made it worse? What do we need to expose, so things can get better?

In relationships, especially those of intimate nature especially those in covenant, one must be able to be totally transparent and unashamed. We must be free enough to allow others to see us in a flawed state without the need to cover up.

In healthy relationships there is no condemnation. Condemnation produces shame. Shame makes one want to hide. It is sad that so many people are hiding in plain sight.

Healthy relationships actively work to create environments where people are okay to be naked and unashamed. In these types of relationships it is okay to be vulnerable because their aim is not to exploit your weakness. These environments thrive on trust, open communication, and a no-judgment zone. This zone is still one of accountability and responsibility but refuses to demand perfection which denies and hinders the process of wholeness.

You, too, can be totally naked. It is a process to take off all the stuff that we have used to cover up our weaknesses, but it's worth it to be free. Whoever my husband is will now be able to see me buck ball naked with the lights on literally and figuratively because I am no longer ashamed of who I am.

I still have some things to work on, but I am no longer allowing perfection to be a state of no flaws. I embrace that I am perfectly flawed, and my flaws serve a purpose in GOD's hands and His plans. Are you okay being totally naked?

Something To Think About

1. What is your cover-up?

2. Do you have a healthy way of processing other people's opinions of you?

3. Is there any dysfunction that influences how you see yourself?

4. What mirror do you look in? Is it man's perception or GOD's intention?

4

KISS ME, PLEASE

Kissing is amazing. The right kiss can do sublime things. I thoroughly enjoy kissing. I could kiss all day. Full beautiful lips that have been cultivated in the art of kissing is another one of GOD's little blessing.

I stand confident that I could just kiss. It has been brought to my attention, though I may be able to kiss all day and stay with kissing, he (the other part to the equation) may not be likewise obliged to observe those boundaries.

But I still had hope. I even prayed, no joke, I prayed to GOD to just give me a kissing partner. All we would do is kiss. He didn't have to be THE ONE, because I just wanted to kiss. I settled and lessened my request from an ongoing kissing partner to GOD; just give me a kiss.

REAL talk, I could have easily gotten a kiss on my own, there were quite a few willing men who would have been honored for the role of my kissing partner. However, my discriminate tastes didn't just want anyone, I wanted someone approved for the task.

I prayed this prayer a couple of times. Don't judge me! At the time, I thought it was a credible, valid prayer. I was going to GOD because He could send the one who could just handle kissing.

On a Sunday many, many moons ago, when I was walking up a choir stand, I passed a brother. As usual, we went to kiss on the cheek in greeting and accidentally kissed on the lips. It was an awkward moment which we tried to laugh off, and we kept it moving.

As I continued to ascend the steps, I heard GOD say, almost as if joking "there was your kiss." I fumed inwardly because that was definitely not the kiss I desired. Continued contemplation gave me pause because I recognized that I may not have been ready for what I prayed for.

Kissing for me is very intimate. It requires an intimate connection. Though I desired that level of intimacy, I can't say I was ready for to be connected to the level of that responsibility.

I once received a prophesy that GOD was getting my order ready, referring to my husband, and it was taking a while because it was a custom order.

So when I received that great prophecy about my order being customized 10 years ago, I was not really encouraged. My immediate response to GOD was, "cool if you are getting my order ready can a sister get an appetizer" and He quickly replied, "your appetizer may spoil the meal, do you still want it?". I came back with a "Nah, I think I will pass."

For some, this type of exchange with GOD sounds strange and very uncommon. My relationship with GOD is one that has been developed through honest conversation and expression. It wasn't always like that because somebody told me not to ask questions. Some said asking GOD questions meant one didn't trust Him. A faulty perception of GOD made me feel like it was disrespectful to express any negative feelings with GOD.

This mindset was checked on one occasion when I had a horrible situation happen and was just giving GOD praise. He responded to my showmanship, saying He could handle my anger. GOD explained that I didn't have to hide or nor hold back anything from Him. He instructed me that before I build an altar, I needed to tear down the stronghold. In other words, be real and deal with it and not just praise on top of it.
That was a very liberating conversation.

After the accidental kiss happened, my thoughts came to that prophetic word. Could my desire for a kissing partner mess up the meal?
Proverbs 27:7 says to the hungry soul even the bitter than is sweet, but the full will loathe even the honeycomb.

I didn't want to be so hungry for a relationship that I took just anything. Was I allowing myself to walk into a set-up like Esau because of a hunger that I couldn't appease?   I had to ask some hard questions. What did kissing represent to me, and why was it so important.   Even as a youth, kissing was high on the scale of intimacies. Shockingly so, you could feel my behind but couldn't kiss me.

Kissing was an exchange. The qualifications for that exchange was a little more discriminatory that just a slight hit on the behind. An exchange is what I was truly desiring. For me, kissing represented a relationship. I only kissed guys that I was in relationship. Though I said I only wanted a kissing partner, I really wanted an approved deserving exchange.

Often, we lie to ourselves and others about what we really want. We use labels and languages to hide our vulnerabilities. The truth was I wanted more than just a kissing partner, I wanted a life partner, and I wasn't willing to settle for something fleeting when I wanted something for forever.

Thoughts of a Virgin

I still enjoy kissing but not to the detriment or dismissal of my other needs. Not every good kisser is a good keeper.

Something To Think About

1. Are you hungry for a relationship?

2. Are you willing to let an appetizer spoil the meal?

3. Do you know what you really want and are you ready for it?

5
THE CHASTITY BELT
FROM HELL

I was 10 years old when they pushed a boy on top of me and told us to "do it." My panic caused me to scream out, "no I don't want to have sex now, I want to be a virgin until I am 11,12, 13, 14, 15, 16, ..." The counting stopped when they pulled the other young boy off me.

The whole group of children ranged in ages from 12-15. I was the youngest. I had skipped two grades, so my peers were typically older than me. They laughed hysterically at the episode. For them, I am sure they considered it nothing serious. Though we were both fully clothed, the fear I felt that day left me exposed, vulnerable, and helpless. Feeling the weight of him on me caused my heart to race as my pushing was inadequate to get him off. Images of rape scenes from afternoon specials were being played in my thoughts.

As I stood up, I laughed it off in my typical fashion, not wanting to bring attention to myself. At that age, I wasn't connected enough with my emotions to recognize the effect of that moment or to stand up for myself.

My childhood was surrounded with an abnormal amount of sexual awareness and activity. Our after school activities were consumed with girls and boys "hunching." This is where the children simulated sex with their clothes on. Though as a child, I never participated, I was still exposed to it.

At a young age, I recall my mother explaining sex to me in a very scientific manner. My mother was very open about sex and procreation. She was open to our questions. Which made me the sex awareness spokesman bringing correction to youthful fallacies at our Christian school.

Often the other girls would try to make me feel bad because I was not sexually active like them. These 10 and 11year old girls were bragging about having sex. Understanding that hunching wasn't sex, I recall using my knowledge to burst their bubbles.

There was time, a girl said she had sex with her boyfriend, and I asked her very bluntly if he inserted his penis into her vagina. The look on her face was priceless. She turned up her lips and screeched, "oooh noo." My response of victory wasn't withheld but released immediately with satisfied glee, "well, you are a virgin just like me." How you like those apples.

I was raised by a Christian mom who lived CHRIST before us in such faithfulness in integrity. She reinforced our need to represent well. She raised us to be leaders, and being a leader meant being mindful of our choices and opportunities. She reminded us that every time we walked out the doors, we should represent 3 people with excellence. GOD, Her as a mother and my race.

I sometimes struggled to perform because I didn't want to let anyone down. I created unrealistic expectations for myself. The responsibility of being the church girl worked well for me until it didn't.

I was afraid to let people down. The need to be perfect pressurized my decisions and at times had an adverse effect. It wasn't a big surprise to discover fear was an underlying reason for my virginity. I shared with you an original episode with a boy. Fear had become my chastity belt from hell.

My mother was very prophetic, like scary prophetic. Those unfamiliar with the word prophetic may be able to relate to those who people say have the "sight." She would know the details of my life and those around me that I never shared. My mother's prophetic ability was so keen that I believed that if I were to try to have sex, HOLY SPIRIT would give her the number to the room, the address if needed, and she meet me at my desired location even before I got there.

You may think I am exaggerating, but I am not. There would be times I would try and make a plan, and she would somehow gather the necessary intel by HOLY SPIRIT to always thwart my plans.

Her intel didn't end with me but included my connections and associations. There was one time when I had a friend who was a virgin like me. One day, out of the blue, my mother shared with me to tell her to be careful.

"Mom, what do you mean?", I responded in confusion,

She replied, she is having sex, tell her to be careful.

I responded, no, mom, she is still a virgin. They are doing "things," but they haven't had sex.

She said, "oh, ok, watch what I tell ya."

The very next day, I ask my friend if she had sex yet. She started blushing and responded, "yes, last week."

My mouth dropped. My friend asked me how did I know. I said I didn't, my mom did.

My life was one that I couldn't get away with anything. It was like I was marked. I could be in a group of youth, and I will be the one singled out for doing the same thing everyone else was doing. Time and time again, if I did it I would be the one to get caught.

I knew I had a call on my life and that the enemy wanted to jack that up irreversibly, so in my mind, I would be the one whose partner had two condoms on, and I still get pregnant. Or the first time I have sex, something goes wrong. I get an STD or AIDS. Many times, after making a plan, I would get some warning. One of my friends would pop up pregnant, break up with the dude right after they just had sex or other many signs. The scenarios ranged far and wide, all with results that I didn't desire. My mother always said if you can't handle the worst-case scenario happening, then don't do it because anything can happen.

My fear of getting caught, kept me a virgin for a long time. But the closer my relationship with CHRIST, the more I didn't want to have sex out of wedlock even if I could get away with.

Do you know how many people appear to be getting away with it with no current consequences? I realized if fear was the only thing keeping me from having sex, my stand was pretty weak.

It was within that time I discovered my reason as to why I didn't want to have sex outside of marriage. Some may be wondering if I ever dealt with the incident when I was 10. I did. The most significant factor of that event was that I felt my choice was taken away from me. I was being forced to do something I didn't want to do. But allowing fear to be the reason I didn't have sex, was permitting that cycle of pressure to continue. What was your first encounter with sex? Was it under duress? Did you enter into the experience with full control, or did you feel some pressure to do it?

Originally, fear was my reason for not having sex. Is fear your reason for having sex? Are you afraid that if you don't have sex in your relationship, you don't have anything? Are you worried that they would leave? Is fear playing a role in your current relationship?

Just as I had to face my fears, I would encourage you to face yours. Fear is never a reason to do or not do anything. For those who are thinking "what about the fear of the LORD"? That fear is not I am afraid of You, LORD but I am in such awe and reverence of you, I don't want to hurt you, not I am so scared you will hurt me.

My stand is not because I don't have a choice. My virginity is not being forced on me. I don't feel like I am being forced not to have sex. Not having sex is my choice.

Sex has the ability to blindfold people from real issues. Removing the confusion that sex sometimes brings allows me to better evaluate relationships in real-time without romantic delusions and make sober decisions.

When I evaluate what I really want out of a relationship, my current approach has proven to be the most effective and in line with what I believe.

Is your approach towards sex and relationships getting what you really? If not, I would challenge you to try a new strategy. What do you think?

Something To Think About

1. Is it fear or commitment that restrains you from having sex?

2. The presence of fear is proof that a lie has been believed.

3. What messages from your youth to even now have shaped your view on sex, masturbation, and /or pornography?

6
THIS IS THE LAST TIME, I PROMISE

Secret struggle and secret shame. The guilty pleasure that once stalked me had become my friend. Its visits became more frequent, and its departure more condemning. I wanted it to leave, but it kept coming back. I cringed every time I thought our relationship would go public, but the embarrassment wasn't enough for me to leave it alone. This toxic relationship kept me in bondage for years. My on and off again affair lasted for over 17 years. After repeated failed attempts to leave this relationship cold turkey, I finally arrived at a place where continuing our relationship would cost me everything.

My secret relationship was with masturbation and pornography. I was introduced masturbation at an early age.

Another young child showed me their newfound understanding. I recall not being aware of what or why they were doing it and didn't try it out myself until a couple of years later. It was only after being molested at 11 did I pick up the habit. This nasty habit put a temporary smile on my face and long-term stains on my heart.

Nobody had to tell me it was wrong. Before ever having a conversation about it, I had the conviction. I would feel bad. The conviction I had was strong but not strong enough.

Years later, I recall going to a Christian event. The speaker mentioned the wrongs of masturbation and boldly, with much hesitation, went up to the front with my youth leader to openly repent to GOD and share with someone my struggle. She prayed with me, and that was it. I don't recall any follow-up or her checking back to how I was faring. I can't blame her. She probably didn't know what to do, few do.

Needless to say, the confession that day didn't win the war. I wasn't ready to share my faults again with a person, so I found myself calling CBN anonymously, asking for prayer. That didn't work either.

Struggling to quit, I started looking for justification to continue. Where in the Bible, does it **actually** say masturbation is a sin? Is it really wrong? Though I continued to play these mind games with myself, I recalled what I thought as a young child witnessing the other child playing with themselves, without anyone ever telling me, I thought it was wrong. I wasn't comfortable though I was curious.

Again, before anyone ever said it was wrong, I felt it was wrong. However, now because I wanted to continue, I started questioning the conviction. Doesn't that sound like what many of us do to be justified? Have you ever done that before?

I can recite the arguments against it. Masturbation is wrong because it was connected to pornographic images of lust and watching others sin. Bam, so what did I do, began masturbating without pornography. My intellectual side moved on to erotica, which I preferred better. There I could create my own characters. The next argument is when you are masturbating, you are thinking about other people, and that was lust. Okay, so I removed the thoughts of others and only concentrated on the feeling I was evoking. Problem solved, yet I still felt convicted.

I remember my futile cries after every interaction, I promised that was the last time only to arrive at the next time.

One day, as I was about to complete the act, I heard HOLY SPIRIT say, what if this is the last time I let you do this. What if I totally take my spirit away from you and you never hear from me again. The life He presented sounded horrid. Though I was by no mean a perfect Christian, one thing steady in my life was my ability to hear from GOD.

I could readily hear the cries of David, whatever you do, please don't take your presence from me. It was easy to imagine the tears of blood CHRIST cried as for the first time, He would be separated from His father.

Though I felt the weight of HOLY SPIRIT words, I was at a crossroads. I had tried by myself for years to stop without success. So what was I to do? It was then I was convinced that I needed outside help.

Though this activity was an enemy to my spirit, it was a beloved friend to my flesh. For the first time, I became willing to have a real conversation with HOLY SPIRIT about why I couldn't stop. He responded, "because you like it. This isn't something that is unpleasant to you. You enjoy it, and you have to be real with your desire for it." He advised that "until you hate it, you won't stop."

According to some, there's an old story about how Natives would put a blade into the ice. A wolf would come and lick the blade. The licking would cut his tongue, but the wolf would continue to lick the blade until he bled to death. It was so engrossed in its desire that it didn't even realize what he was doing was killing himself.

Not all sin feels terrible. Some sin has scintillating upfront benefits. We know on the backend there is death, but when something feels good, it is easy to forget death is around the corner, waiting to snatch you up.

Though I thought I hated it: apparently, I didn't hate it enough. I hated the feeling of guilt but loved the sense of fulfilled desire. My love was stronger than my hate.

James 1:14 says it best "Temptation comes from our own desires, which entice us and drag us away."

Masturbation was dragging me further and further away from what I truly desired, and that was a closer relationship with CHRIST.

I recognized that whatever you feed will always be stronger than what you starve. I had fed my flesh and desires for the perverse more than I had fed my spirit, so in this tug of war, my flesh was ultimately stronger.

I had to learn how to starve my flesh and feed my spirit. In my opinion, change begins with responsibility and accountability. I first started this journey by confessing to my mother that I was struggling in this area. This was huge for me because my mother had a very high opinion of me and I didn't want to let her down,

I recall in delight that the conversation didn't go like I thought it would. I called her up and shared my struggle, and she didn't flinch. She asked me if I repented, I said yes and asked what was I going to do about it and what could she do to help me. No shame was given, I felt no condemnation. I replied, honestly with an "I don't know."

But James 1:14 kept coming to mind. I had to change my desires. That began by first changing what I allowed in my eye and ear gates. I use to watch shows like Sex in the City. Each scene heavily laden with sex and sexual overtones. I lied to myself and said I only watch it for the fashion. Deception can cover the doors of freedom. I was also an avid reader of romance novels and even erotica. I threw away all my books and stopped watching television for a season while I built myself up.

I went to Scripture for perspective. Psalms 119:9 asked and answered my question of how? "How can a young man cleanse his way? By taking heed according to Your word."

I started doing Word searches in Scripture. Topics like self-control, thoughts, and strongholds were very instrumental. I recall praying consistently, LORD let me love what you love and hate what you hate.

Every time a thought would come, I would use 2 Corinthians 10:5 KJV "Casting down imaginations, and every high thing that exalteth itself against the knowledge of God, and bringing into captivity every thought to the obedience of Christ;"

I did this religiously. The struggle was real. I recall hearing a pastor say something, that for me was the game-changer. He shared how he changed his thoughts by casting a thought down within 5 seconds.

By adding this piece, thoughts that before were quite frequent, stop appearing as much. I wasn't aware of how often I had sexual thoughts. In the beginning, I was using that Scripture sometimes 20 times a day. But after I started using the 5-second rule, my thoughts would not have as many repeats.

Thoughts are like seeds, and if you allow them enough time, they will reproduce. I had to kill it in its seed form and uproot so it would not be able to reap a harvest.

This wasn't an easy or overnight battle. There were tests along the way. One time stands out, I was in the library, and they had an erotic novel for only 10 cents. I did contemplate the purchase. HOLY SPIRIT arrested me by asking, "is your soul only worth 10 cents?". Way to put things in perspective. What was I about to give up for 10 cents? What have you given up?

It was those real-life battles that made me appreciate those I had in my corner. I got an accountability partner. I shared my struggle with a person from my church. When the feeling got overwhelming, and I needed help, she would talk me down from the ledge and keep me distracted until the feeling past. One thing I discovered is, the feeling always passed.

In the beginning it was hard. I never forget one time, I ran out of my house and sat on the porch. I didn't want to give myself any excuses. I removed all possibility of me falling. Some say it doesn't take all that, that day for me it did. Previously for me, masturbation was an addiction. It was something I couldn't say no to. Understanding its roots and its rituals, I had to be aggressive with my approach.

The changes I implemented allowed December 2004 to be the last time I masturbated. Yay!! Yet I still can't get comfortable. I still have to be diligent. In 2012, the beast tried to come back, but this time though pornographic anime. One time, an ad came on one of the shows I was watching online. Though the show was g rated and didn't have kissing in it, the ad that came on had much more than kissing. I watched it a second too long and ended up watching more than I should. Justification tried to come in again. This time my excuse because it was anime, and they weren't real people; it wasn't as bad. I caught myself about to lose everything I had gained and reached out to my accountability team and shared the struggle. We prayed. I repented and reinforced boundaries.

The next night I had a dream where a monster was in what appeared to be a princess room. Its décor was very girlie and innocent. All the furniture was white. The carpet was white. There was a soft pink lamp and bedspread. A monster came in looking for something. He was rummaging through drawers and looking under the bed. He let out in a growl and a humph then slammed the door. When the door closed, I heard, "and he found nothing." It reminded me of the Scripture that when the enemy comes, let him find nothing.

If the enemy was to come in right now in your life, what would he find? Is there something in your life that provides him a hiding place. Are there connections that he can latch onto that need to be broken? GOD is not looking for you to be perfect. He knows you inside and out and still loves you. The enemy is merely waiting for you to surrender. It is my constant surrender that fuels a lifestyle that would allow when the enemy comes looking, he finds nothing.

Something To Think About

1. If you struggle with masturbation, what opened the door to this habit?

2. Where has temptation or desire led you astray?

3. What has solo sex robbed you of?

Do you struggle with masturbation/pornography and want help? Email thoughtsofavirgin@gmail.com so we can connect you with tools and strategies to stand victorious.

7
THE EDGE MINISTRY

I admit I am a freak. Combine my exposure to sexual environments/experiences, and my highly sensitive prophetic nature (I will explain the connection to the prophetic at another time), without CHRIST, we have a concoction for trouble. Some would question, how can a virgin be a freak, my prior experiences have demonstrated a voracious sexual appetite. Whoever my husband is, may need to start taking his vitamins now because we will definitely be making up for lost time through fervency and frequency.

I recognized early on that I was very adventurous sexually, but I had my limits. No sex, vaginal, anal, or oral. But there were plenty of other things I was opened to that were sketchy when comparing to holiness. I call that the Edge Ministry. The Edge ministry is defined by taking things to edge and doing everything but actual intercourse.

Living on the edge is for one who is of two opinions. It is being doubleminded. When you live on the edge, you stay in deception. The edge is sneaky and slippery. One of the problems with the edge ministry is when you live on the edge, you are always one step away from falling off.

Growing up, I could only get black, white, or beige bras. Due to size, my bras weren't cheap. I remember once asking my mom for some pretty ones. She bantered back as if I was joking and asked, "why, who's going to see them?". That was the end of that conversation.

Who indeed? At that time, it was my boyfriend who was getting views of my black, white, and beige bras. He had awakened me sexually, which kept me living on the edge. My desire to be sexy for him made me creative. Since I was not able to get what I thought was sexy bras, I put bleach in a spray bottle and sprayed my black bra and panties. It created this cool effect. I was so impressed and ready to show off my design. I must admit he was impressed too. I laugh as I write this because, though my design was cool, it didn't last long, because bleach eats holes in clothes.

The day I showed off my design, I found myself on the edge, edge. One thing about lust, it will ALWAYS take you further than you want to go. Lust had taken my germaphobe self into a nasty bathroom where we were making out with heavy petting and unique maneuvers. I must admit, it wasn't my back against the nasty wall but distinctly remember the bathroom we were in wasn't anyone's example for clean.

I found myself wanting to do things I said I never would. The edge was pulling me until I almost fell off. Nothing but mercy and grace kept my virginity in tack that day. When I got mentally sober, I realized how engulfed I was in lust and desire then was immediately sad. That scenario describes the edge where many are living, doing things they thought they would never do, even things they were once determined never to do.

I had to question, how did I get there? The answer came quickly, compromise.   My bathroom escapade wasn't an overnight result. It was the constant moving of my lines of standard. Standards that before were resolute and unchangeable became more and more flexible and pliable to my desires.

Compromise hovers and lingers looking for openings to kidnap our desires and take them hostage demanding payments that we can't afford. With each payment, we lose more and more of our character and integrity. The thing about compromise is its ability to desensitize us to sin. What before was horrible becomes plausible and even justifiable. Compromise can happen when the purpose of a thing is muddled. For me, my original goal was not to have sex until I was married, so according to that goal, OTHER things were allowed. Many of those things were not in line with fully pleasing GOD. This became painfully obvious back in 2011. I was coming off one mission trip from the Dominican Republic and going into another one in Detroit, Michigan. My very brief pit stop had me in the vicinity of a pastor whose flirtations have been received and returned. There was a strong sexual connection, and we had previously exchanged intimate conversation. He admitted that my status as a virgin was very intriguing to him.

I began the text,
Me: How I wish I could see you.
Him: WHAT!! Are you here? When are you leaving?
Me: I fly out tomorrow
Him: Man. if I could see you, I would....... and goes into very graphic detail to what he would like to do sexually. He had me excited until he added a word of profanity. Which was like cold water on my excitement. I personally find profanity ignorant and very unattractive. That ended up being was my way of escape. GOD can use anything.

I still heeheed and hahaha laughing it off, saying that we couldn't afford to fall together and lose our anointing or our call. It was easy to stand firm because I was no longer excited. That SAME day, I went to a Pastors and Bishops Meeting. After the meeting closed, HOLY SPIRIT told me to show the text to the organizer of the event. He was a more mature saint. With many, he walked in the role of father. My response to HOLY SPIRIT was, "Nah".

I didn't want to expose myself like that but felt if I missed this opportunity I would miss out on something much more. I passed my phone and asked him to read the texts. It appeared to take forever. In my mind, I wondered why I didn't delete the text immediately and tried to recall what was said. What seems like a lifetime passed, he looked up and said, "You know you started this".

I feigned a look of ignorance and asked "huh?". He let me know that there was a motive connected to my reaching out. I agreed. He then asked if I repented, I said yes. I left. Yet when I arrived home, I heard the soft voice of HOLY SPIRIT, He said "I am hurt that you would even play with that," the pain I heard in His remark, brought me to my knees with tears in my eyes. It was then that I understood the term godly sorrow. Before, I was just guilty about my actions, but now I was hurt that I hurt GOD with my actions. The grief was palatable as I cried out with another level of repentance.

It was then that I discovered, just the desire

to not have sex wasn't enough. Simply not having sex allowed inappropriate touching and texting. But a passion for holiness wouldn't. It was then that I started pursuing holiness, not just celibacy. Holiness goes beyond the area of my sex drive. Holiness taps into anything that could pervert my sex drive and expose me to temptations that otherwise could have been easily avoided.

One would think that pursuing holiness would make things harder. Yet pursuing holiness actually made things easier. Placing boundaries and standards in how I dealt with the opposite sex helped me out a lot. Many Christians live on the edge. We entertain things we shouldn't, taking another step in the wrong direction, causing a detrimental fall. A fall that comes with consequences that delay or detour destiny

I believe this is why many famous pastors and Christian leaders fall. What before was a life of pursuing holiness became a life of pursuing platforms. Every platform comes with its own level of enticement and/or character building. If you are already on the edge, one step into one thing is a step out of something else. I have seen many step outside of the bounds of holiness to pursue fame, fortune, and friends.

I beseech you therefore, brethren, by the mercies of God, that ye present your bodies a living sacrifice, holy, acceptable unto God, which is your reasonable service.
Romans 12:1

It is possible to present your bodies including your sex drive as a living sacrifice, and truth be told, it is also reasonable.

Something To Think About

1. Are you living on the edge?

2. How did you get there?

3. What does holiness look like for you?

4. What boundaries do you have in place to honor your commitment to GOD?

8
IS SEX SPIRITUAL

I have heard people describe sex like an out of this world experience. Many have reported orgasmic moments that felt as if they could transport them to other realms. So let me ask you this question, is sex spiritual?

I got a glimpse of sex's spiritual implication when HOLY SPIRIT shared w that when I masturbated, I was opening myself up to spirits. At my moments of orgasm, I was open to intrusion. He shared that at moments of orgasm, we are open and vulnerable, and in His design through marriage, we would be covered by a covenant.

There are those who believe sex is spiritual. Terms such as magic sex and tantric sex allude to sex being spiritual. Even some pagan and wiccan rituals include sex when they require powerful energy. Sex is seen as one of the most potent energy sources. The power is drawn from the connection between the male and the female during the act and used toward willing a specific outcome.

We can see the enemy's use of sex to gain spiritual ground with succubus and incubus. These are spirits whose aim is to get people to engage in sexual activity unawares through dreams and open visions. Many have taken it lightly. I believe that attitude is because of a lack of understanding of the seriousness of the matter.

Scriptures show its stand with these verses:

"and the two will become one flesh.' So they are no longer two, but one flesh." Mark 10:8

Do you not know that the one who joins himself to a prostitute is one body with her? He says, "THE TWO SHALL BECOME ONE FLESH." 1 Corinthians 6:15

I believe we all know the mechanics of sex. For those of us who do, we understand how the physical connection is in play. Yet, there are still two bodies present. How then does one become one?

I believe the oneness mentioned is depicting what happens spiritually. During sex, you become one with the other party. This is how, through that intimate relationship, there is a oneness that starts manifesting that, at times, is unexplainable. Sex impacts the mind, body, and soul. Its power, at times, can intermingle in all three areas causing ripple effects to one's mental and emotional being. This threefold cord is not often easily broken. Sex will influence you without permission. Sex can cause a deception that has put the sanest people under a delusion.

Dr. Daniel Amen writes in his book, "Change Your Brain, Change Your Life," "Whenever a person is sexually involved with another person, neurochemical changes occur in both their brains that encourage limbic, emotional bonding. Limbic bonding is the reason casual sex doesn't really work for most people on a whole mind and body level. Two people may decide to have sex 'just for the fun of it,' yet something is occurring on another level that they might not have decided on at all: sex is enhancing an emotional bond between them whether they want it or not. One person, often the woman, is bound to form an attachment and will be hurt when a casual affair ends. One reason it is usually the woman who is hurt most is that the female limbic system is larger than the male's."

Sex provides a spiritual connection, even when unplanned. One-night stands though the connection is brief still leaves indelible imprints on one's souls. People have made these spiritual connections unknowingly and are now in bondage to things they never imagined. The bondage can result in soul ties.

According to Kris Vallotton, there are 7 ways to determine if you have a soul tie:

1.   You are in a physically and/or emotionally, and/or spiritually abusive relationship, but you "feel" so attached to them that you refuse to cut off the connection and set boundaries with them.

2.   You have left a relationship (maybe long ago), but you think about the other person obsessively (you can't get them out of your mind).

3.   Whenever you do anything – make a decision, have a conversation with someone, etc., you "feel" like this person is with you or watching you.

4.   When you have sex with someone else (hopefully your husband or wife), you can hardly keep yourself from visualizing the other person you have a soul tie with.

5.   You take on the negative traits of the person that your soul is tied to and carry their offenses whether or not you actually agree with them.

6.   You defend your right to stay in a relationship with the person that your soul is tied to, even though it is negatively affecting or even destroying the important relationships in your life (husband, wife, kids, leaders, etc.)

7.   You have simultaneous experiences

and/or "moods" as the person your soul is tied to. This can even include sickness, accidents, addictions, etc.

Breaking a soul tie may be challenging but not impossible. Hopefully, the list below can be helpful in breaking soul ties.

1. **DECIDE**

This is truly the first step. Until you make a decision, there can be no difference. You have to make up in your mind that you no longer want to be connected and that you are willing to do whatever necessary without excuses.

2. **DISCERN**

Discernment is key. Discernment doesn't just show what is wrong; it shows you why it's wrong. Discernment is cultivated through the study of the Scriptures. Connecting with HOLY SPIRIT and asking for revelation and, if necessary, requesting the assistance of another spiritual friend.

3. **DETERMINE**

Now that you have discerned the what and why now we must deal with the how. You must determine what steps you need to take to be free. Does that include blocking numbers, changing numbers, or even changing routes that included a drive-by to see if he/she was home?

4. **DESTROY/DELETE**

It is recommended that you destroy memorabilia connected to that person. Letters, texts, jewelry (For the most part, I personally have no problem with selling jewelry. Be led by HOLY SPIRIT to see if that is an option for you) pictures, stuff animals, perfumes. All of those things can serve as a connection to that person.

5. **DISCONNECT**

Say a prayer of disconnection.

Heavenly Father,
I come to You now. Thank You for loving me. Thank You that continue to prove Your love for me that even while I was still in sin, You provided an answer to my situations. Your

Word says You came to set the captives free. I confess that _____ has captivated me. I have chosen them over You. I repent and ask for Your forgiveness for and sins resulting from this connection. My connection to them has affected my heart, mind, and body and placed me in spiritual bondage. I truly desire to be free.

I cancel every lie and deception that allowed this tie to remain. I desire truth in my inward parts. I ask HOLY SPIRIT to try my heart and see if there be any hidden thing that would give this soul tie a hiding place. I speak that everything hidden is revealed and removed. Any spirits of lust or perversion that were fed through this connection, I renounce it now and uproot it from its hold. I thank You that You are a GOD of love, and I receive that love to flood my empty places and keep me filled and untouchable to return visits.

Your Word says that whom the Son sets free is free indeed. Today I claim that freedom. I cancel known and unknown alliances that I made with _____ through sex, intimate interactions, conversations, thoughts, and gifts. I refuse any and all negative manipulations and influences from that connection. I use the Sword of the Spirit to sever those connections and cancel their ability to reconnect.

I decree and declare that this is a new day, and I receive the new thing You desire for my life in this area. Teach me how to walk this thing out daily with success. I accept your grace and power to live this out in JESUS CHRIST name, we live love and pray. Amen

Something To Think About

1. Do you think sex is spiritual?

2. Do you have a soul tie?

3. Do you believe you need deliverance? Are you willing to fight for it?

It is our desire to set the captive free.

Contact us at:

thoughtsofvirgin@gmail.com

9
EMBRACING TRUTH

I think we have approached this sex thing wrong, especially within the body of CHRIST. We have placed demands on people who haven't been equipped with that capacity to meet those demands. We have told people repeatedly, DON'T HAVE SEX, DON'T HAVE SEX, but failed to empower people to live out that possibility in a healthy way. What tools or strategies have we given? What type of conversations have we started? I want to start a conversation!!

Sometimes a conversation is all that is needed to open up a path of understanding that transforms lives. I mentored girls for years. Many of my jobs connected me with youth. I worked as a Program Director at a youth center, and the girls would gravitate to me. Saved or not saved, they knew if they wanted to hang out with me over the weekend, we were going to church, and they still wanted to come. I knew what the girls were dealing with at home, so I didn't mind the many requests. I wanted them to know what a safe place looked like. On this particular occasion, I had 2 young ladies with me. We were eating at McDonald's. It was our place of choice because of their dollar menu. I was only working part-time, so money was tight, and this way, each girl could at least still get three things off the menu.

The young ladies were 12 and 13 years old. They started sharing about their boyfriends, and I allowed them to speak uninterrupted. The 13 year-old nudged the 12 year-old and said: "tell Ms. Idella, go ahead, tell her." I responded with, "tell me what." The 12 year-old was silent, but the 13year-old couldn't hold her peace. She blurted out, "Tell Ms. Idella that you are having sex." I had been trained at how to deal with youth when talking about sex, so I was sure that my face showed no shock or judgment. We then began a conversation. During that conversation, we discovered her why. Understanding her why allowed me to challenge her understanding to arrive at another conclusion. We arrived at that conclusion without shame, judgment, or ridicule.

She, too, had been exposed to sex early on. I shared how I was molested by a family friend. For me to embrace the beauty of sex, I had to deal with that ugly episode. So many people's views of sex have been tainted by force or persuasion. We rarely give time and space for people to arrive and deal with their truths. When we beat people over the head with our judgment, it makes one defensive. People rarely tell you the truth when they are defensive. It is the truth that sets one free, without truth, there is no opening for freedom.

I recall wanting to do a "Purity Conference" for young ladies with purity rings, and HOLY SPIRIT said no, it won't be practical for my audience. He told me that instead of a purity conference, have an "Embracing Truth" Conference. He advised that many people can't even wrap their minds around purity. Within our cultures, their experiences and possible lifestyles have been so far removed from "purity" that the concept would be foreign. Our culture romanticizes sex. It places an unrealistic expectation of sex. It is used in positions and roles out of order.

For some reason, some people believe sex is going to make everything better. They have been deceived by temporary feelings and even told lies by their abusers. He told me to teach the girls who attended how to embrace the truth. The why behind it. When the why is confronted by the truth, decisions can change.

I once worked with this creamy dark chocolate brother with long dreads, there was a mutual attraction. Since I was in management and he was a rep, we never entertained anything.

However, one day, he came into the restaurant that I was and said that he thought he saw me and had to come in to speak. Since we no longer worked together, we exchanged numbers and decided to have dinner one night. He came over, I cooked and we ended the night with a great hug. You know the type of hugs where you are embraced from head to toe. The attraction was stronger than before. His mere voice could excite me to ovulation. We made plans for him to come over again. I, in a moment of sexual excitement, made the statement to GOD, if he comes over tonight, I am going to have sex. This brotha looked like he truly would know what He was doing.

Long story short, he didn't come over that night. He called 2 days later, truly apologetic because he wanted to come but couldn't find my number. He didn't know why he couldn't find it in his phone but found it later underneath his dresser. He commented on how strange it was. I knew it wasn't unusual, but divine intervention once again. He was trying to set up another time to come. I said no, because those 2 days gave me time to sit in my truth. The truth was I really didn't like the guy enough to pursue a relationship. I just wanted the attention he gave. We didn't have much in common other than lust. I was saved from making a decision that I would have genuinely regretted.

Truth comes out in some very interesting ways. In 2009, I was on an extended fast, 40 days. During this fast, I hosted daily prayer calls, Every day at either 12a or 6a, it rotated. It was a fantastic time. On this particular day, there was something amuck. I was entertaining a flirtation. I called him my Arabian Night. He was so fine that I gave him a pass on my usual height requirements of 6' or higher and was totally at peace with his 5'9 frame. He was intelligent, humorous, and spiritual (not saved). Our conversations were always insightful, engaging, and scintillating. This day, we had begun a discussion with witty innuendos and risqué questions. Though the subject was consistently mild, his ability to challenge me cerebrally with well thought out details had me hot and bothered. Our interchange was interrupted by work demands, so I told him we would finish it when I got home.

This was years before I got hit with the godly sorrow. I arrived home, anticipating the continuation of the conversation. My heat was interrupted by HOLY SPIRIT with some truth that was like cold water. He posed this question "So what are you going do? Talk dirty, and then what? You don't want to masturbate (which I didn't), so what are you going do? Just be hot, bothered, and have wet panties, then have to do a prayer call." The reality of what I was contemplating hit me hard in the face. What type of foolishness was that? Needless to say, I repented and chose to take my happy hips to sleep and later led the prayer call with no condemnation, free to fully flow. I received a testimony that it was that call that inspired someone to make a decision that changed her life for good.

It was facing the truth that allowed me to make a different decision. Many within the church have not been provided safe environments to deal with their truth. Somethings need to be said to be understood. As a pastor, I am determined to change the narrative.

Society has created this belief that if you are over a certain age and still a virgin or celibate, there must be something wrong with you. The crazy thing is this thought is even within church settings. Society has painted the picture that not having sex isn't healthy, and abstinence is for right-wing fanatics or groups of people who never cut their hair, can't wear pants, and must look homely to be holy. The mere thought that if you aren't having sex means something is wrong with you promotes the mindset that sex is a tool to fix things and/or people. Those who have co-signed to ever realistically addressing the problem.

Sex isn't a fix to ones' brokenness. If it were, we wouldn't see so many dysfunctional relationships with great sex between them. Or so many broken people who are having great sex. Do you get what I am saying?

I want to open up the dialogue. I first want to start off this conversation with the understanding, WITHIN ITSELF THERE IS NOTHING WRONG WITH BEING A VIRGIN OR BEING ABSTINENT. Just ensure your motives are balanced and coming from a healthy place. I have encountered some who are sexually active being they are repressed not because of their relationship with CHRIST.

Sex can't now or ever fill one's brokenness. Only GOD can provide that kind of peace. Understanding this will save you countless hours of pain, tears, and frustration. Sex is good, and its designed environment should be freely and wholeheartedly celebrated, but until then, I am wonderful with waiting.

Prayerfully, this book has given you a lot to think about. I desire that you read something that caused you to enter into conversations of self-discovery and cultivation. If you too decide that you want to wait until marriage please know, that there is nothing wrong with you either, and it's never too late to start doing it GODs way!

Something To Think About
1. What truth do you need to embrace to be free?

2. Has anyone placed sexual demands on you that robbed you of your freedom?

3. What forgiveness needs to be given and received to be totally free?

ABOUT THE AUTHOR

Idella Liselle is interestingly different. She refuses to fit into molds of tradition that serve no purpose. Idella believes challenging the status quo is why she was created.

She is a mogul in the making. Known as The CEO Coach, her passion is to connect people with Purpose, Power & Profit! She serves as the Chief Spiritual Officer of Idella Liselle Companies, Enterprises and Organizations. She developed Kairos Coaching Institute where she certifies life coaches who deal with the natural and the spiritual.

She also serves as Lead Pastor to REAL Ministries. An online ministry dedicated to providing a safe place for people to be healed, whole, encounter CHRIST for REAL and change the world.

She spends her free time creating beautiful spaces through interior design and repurposing furniture which is one of her favorite hobbies.

Contact Information
770-727-1NOW
ThoughtsofaVirgin@gmail.com
www.idellaliselle.com
www.REALMinistryInstitute.org
www.PublishHer.org

BECOME AN AUTHOR

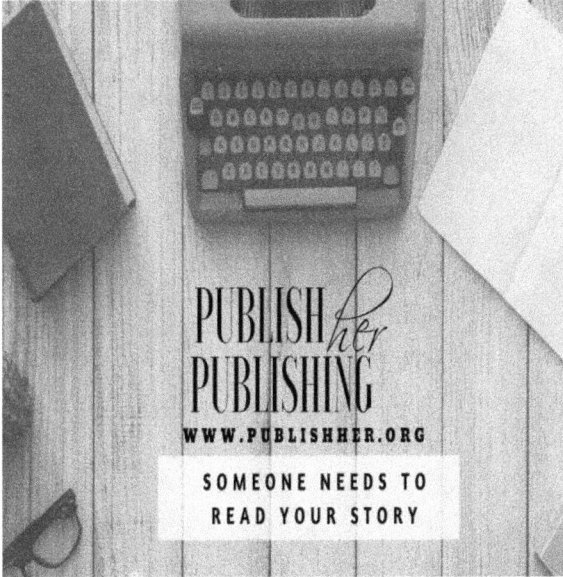

Publish*her* is looking for authors for its next

compilation. Has challenges made your life interesting? Do you have a story to tell? Would you like to be an author in our next compilation or have a book you need assistance in publishing? We would love to bring your story to life. Contact us today!

For more information, go to www.publishher.org.

Idella Liselle

IS CHURCH KILLING YOU?
SURVIVING MINISTRY

Idella
McIntyre
Foreword by Pastor Riva Tims

BOOK EXCERPT
Is Church Killing You? Surviving Ministry

Deception can only be effectively played on the stage of life if you have the leading role.

The Art of Deception

"And He said, Go and tell this people, Hear ye indeed but understand not; and see ye indeed, but perceive not. Make the heart of this people fat, and make their ears heavy, and shut their eyes; lest they see with their eyes; lest they hear with their ears, and understand with their heart and convert and be healed." Isaiah 6:9-10(KJV)

Whenever you identify church hurt there is a connecting thread of deception. In my experience with church hurt, I saw a deception in man which opened my eyes to the other deception around me and an even greater deception within me.

My encounter with deception brought amazing discoveries. I was determined to never be deceived again. I even purchased a book called, Never Be Lied to Again. I was challenged to know what was real from what was

Memorex. What was the church that GOD wanted me to experience, and what was the church that I had created through opinions and excuses of man? I was being inducted into a church that allowed people to lead with no consequences to sin, error, or accountability. I was a faithful member of the church of humanity. It sounds strange when announced like that, but are you a member?

This church stands with the statement of faith that we are only human. This excuses the accountability that comes with Christian living and leadership within the Body of CHRIST. I am not denying the frailties that lie within each and every one of us, but when did it become okay to answer sin with excuses that tout a don't-judge-me message? Where are the screams of a brokenness that acknowledges, "I was wrong and I want to be restored"? Where is the restored leadership that becomes transparent with a determination that will bear all so that the trap and proclivities that claim hundreds and even thousands at their sin have a voice crying in the wilderness that there is a better way?

Deception is strong and strategic to the

church hurt festering in the Body of CHRIST. Often, the fact is, no one wants to deal with the reality of our conditions, and because of the implications of truth, they choose to rest in the comfort of being deceived. If I claim I don't see it, then what responsibility do I have to deal with it? According to the Macmillan Dictionary, deception is defined as the act of deceiving or being deceived. Deception is a dual poison. It cannot be given without being received. Deception is a tool that is often implemented by the devil with the ultimate purpose to stop the conversion and healing of a person. The enemy understands that if he can lock us up in lies, we will never be set free. John 8:32 (KJV) states, "And you shall know the Truth and the Truth will set you free."

In intercession for the Body of CHRIST, GOD challenged me to pray against deception. This question of deception plagued me and caused me to seek GOD for greater understanding. The question that challenged me was how one gets entangled in deception. I use the word, "entangled," because deception is like a web that locks us into a position and stops our spiritual momentum. As I was looking outward to find my answers, an inner tug told me that my search need not go too far. During a session in prayer, GOD showed me a vision of a wash bucket with spiders floating on the top. I immediately understood the revelation but simultaneously assumed that this was for someone else. I boasted to my mom that GOD was washing someone of deception. I did so with the mention of someone else's name and she then challenged me with the question, "Could it be you that GOD is washing you of deception?"

An immediate defense entered. "Not me!" I thought, "I am righteous. I fast and pray. I seek GOD continually." My defense was an alarm that help was needed. I earnestly sought GOD to understand what He was saying. On the first approach to this subject, I could readily see how other mighty men and women of GOD were deceived by looking at them. Their many actions and continuing erroneous stand told me that we could not be reading and understanding the same Scriptures. I could easily point fingers and stand on my righteous soapbox, yell until the cows came home, and rant about the deceit and treachery that I witnessed at the hands of those who claimed titles of the most spiritual elite. Yet it was my own heart that had grown

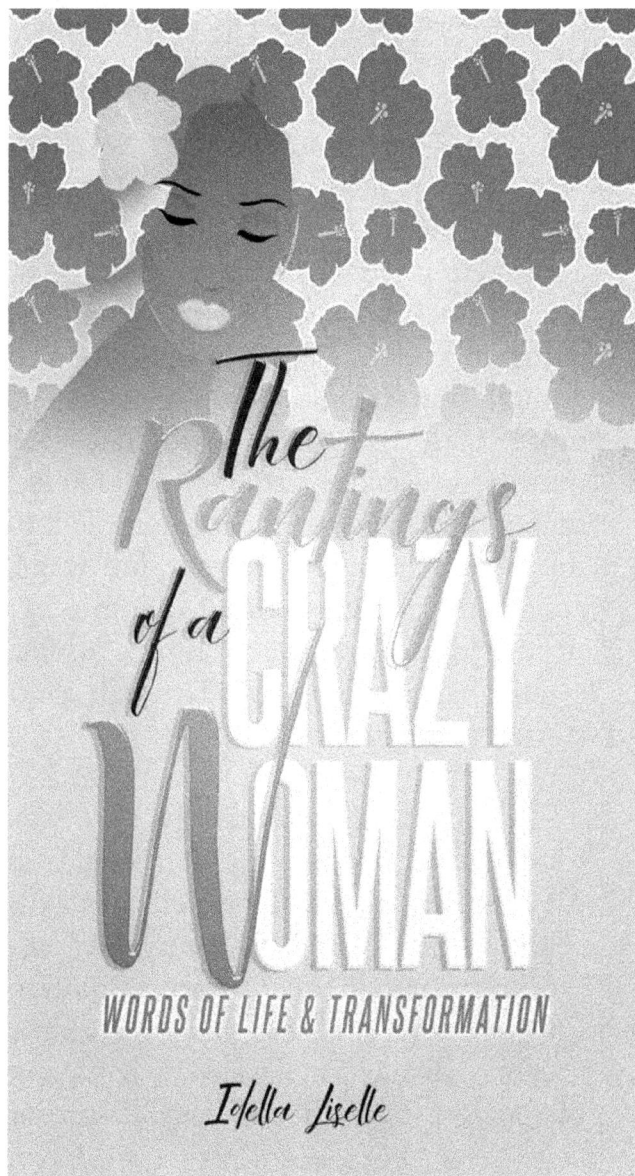

The Rantings of a CRAZY WOMAN

WORDS OF LIFE & TRANSFORMATION

Idella Liselle

BOOK EXCERPT
RANTINGS OF A CRAZY WOMAN

WELCOME TO MY WORLD

Welcome to my world - one that is consistently crazy! During the compilation of these stories, I was in an interesting place. I was going to church with a smile on my face but coming home thinking that there has got to be more than this. Don't get me wrong. My ministry was taking off, but it still felt like a walk that should have been a run. People looking on the outside thought that my life was peaches and cream, which is fine for some, but GOD promised me strawberry shortcake. I was very aware that this is not it! Through that time, I started getting distracted.

This distraction was deadly. It consumed my focus and retarded my stride. It could have been catastrophic if left unchecked. It was the dark shadow that clouded my sunny days, constantly lurking around, demanding my attention.

This distraction was not a man. My distraction was called "lack", spiritual lack, emotional lack, physical lack, financial lack, and relational lack. I allowed it to announce itself on every level. As I looked at the vision that I was to run and how ill-equipped I was, I began to panic. My panic led to frustration and then inner turmoil. I was looking at the picture of my destiny, trying to decipher the many colors. The colors started bleeding and blending to the point I did not know where one color stopped and another began. It was tiring.

No one knew. Being saved for a considerable amount of time allows for some very skilled performances. We know what to say and how to act. I had it down pat. I can minister to you and you never know that I was hurting. I found it hard to trust others to handle my pain, so I masked it beyond excellent service. Mind you, the service isn't fake; it is genuine but hollow.

I found it easy to believe the LORD for others. For others, I can tear down walls and leap over troops. I will fight for them. But very seldom did I find it easy to fight for me. I would put my needs on the back burner until I smelled smoke. What was in the pot to serve hungry people became inedible. Reverently afraid of making someone sick because of ill-prepared food, I stopped cooking my food and just assisted others with their meal.

It is easy to hide behind the crowd. But when GOD is calling one to lead, the need for obedience becomes crucial because the reality is, someone is waiting for your obedience.

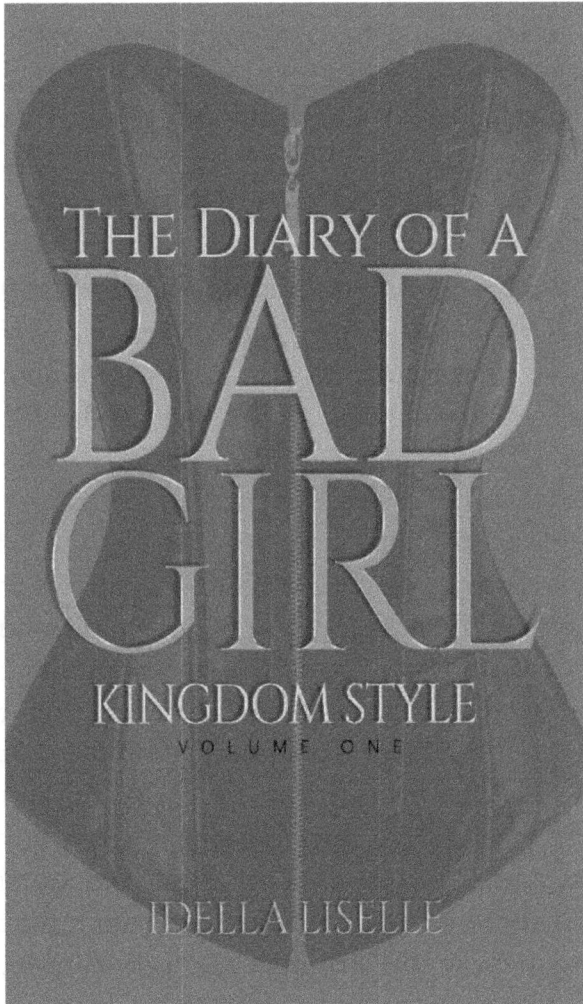

BOOK EXCERPT
FROM DIARY OF A BAD GIRL

BAD ON PURPOSE

But as for you, you meant evil against me; but GOD meant it for good, in order to bring it about as it is this day, to save many people alive.   *Genesis 50:20*

Have you ever felt like life had it in for you? I mean, even from birth, you felt like the odds were always stacked against you. These thoughts almost breed a sense of helplessness. The next thing we know is that we are living a life braced for impact, always expecting the other shoe to drop. To add salt to injury, a lack of a healthy foundation in early childhood allows for endless questioning of self- worth, value, and   purpose. Those on the outside would think that it was a setup for failure, but through more discerning eyes, one can see a masterful plan set in play, favored to have some interesting challenges in my life. At a young age, I knew there was something different about me.

Thoughts of a Virgin

My dreams weren't the typical child's dreams.

While other children were dreaming of rainbows and lollipops, I was having dreams of fighting witches and warlocks. I was dreaming of saving drowning people or saving children, men, and women from buildings on the verge of collapsing.

I remember sharing some of those dreams in gory detail with my mother and her encouraging me that I had power even in my dreams. She told me to use the name of JESUS and that I was able to do anything in my dreams. That piece of information was the game changer. No longer was I being tormented in my dreams. The fear was gone. Now, no matter what tried to appear, I knew I was powerful. I would fly in my dreams and walk on water in my dreams. Even as a child, I knew that there were some places where I could be unstoppable.

As for my dream space, I had that down, but my waking moments still had their bout of issues. At an early age, I was introduced to perversion. I was first shown how to touch myself at 7 by another little girl at daycare. Then I saw my first pornographic magazine at the age of 9 with my brother and some neighborhood boys. At the age of 11, I was molested by a female family friend who had probably also been molested. The trap was set.

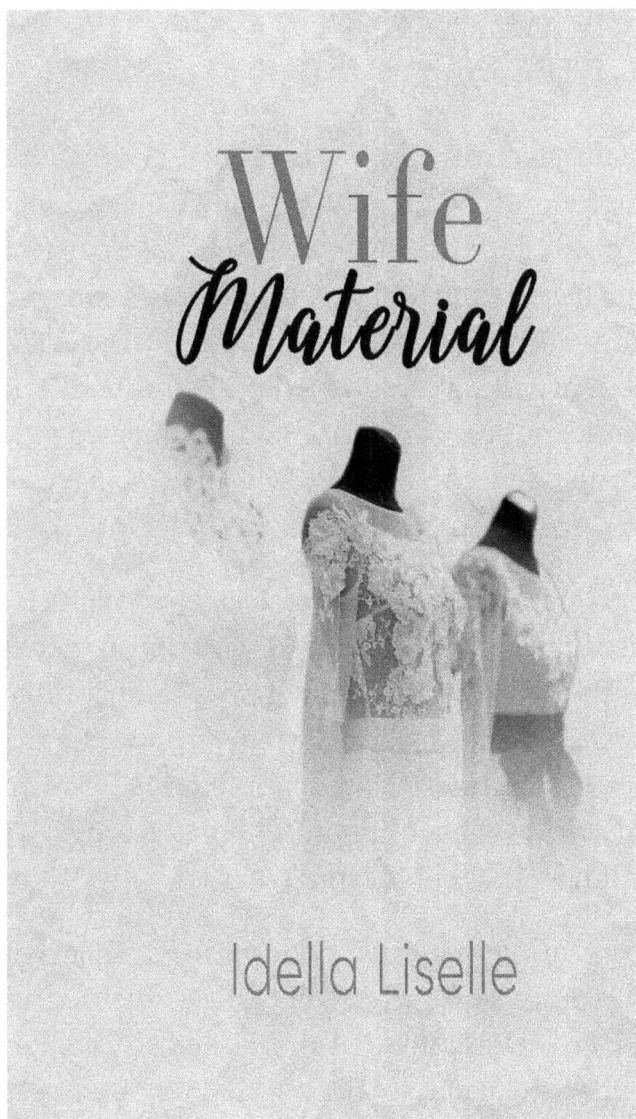

Wife
Material

Idella Liselle

BOOK EXCERPT
WIFE MATERIAL

In my early 20s, I was obsessed with getting married. In fact, I actually think it started when I was a little younger than that. Marriage was my destination and my completion. In my daily conversation and contemplation, all roads led to marriage. I can now admit that much of the earlier appeal of marriage was connected to my strong desire to have sex. I wanted to have sex, and for me, marriage was the only option.

I fantasized about marriage, romanticized about marriage. Marriage would connect me with my Prince Charming, my personal rescue. I wholeheartedly bought that famous line from Jerry McGuire: "You Complete Me." For me, marriage would right all my wrongs and connect me with destiny.

During that time, I connected with a group of young ladies whose end game was marriage as well. Our conversations would all begin and end with "when we get married this, and I can't wait to get married to do that." For a while, this seemed quite normal. Even sermons and messages seemed to promote marriage as a prerequisite to be effective in the Kingdom. Whether directly or indirectly, the message that destiny isn't fulfilled without marriage was being pushed.

This pushed my obsession into overdrive. Every eligible bachelor I met came with the question, "could he be it?" It started to create a neediness in me that was not a good look. This neediness started repelling what I desired and attracted what I did not want. This cycle went uninterrupted for a while.

I continued to believe the fairy tale that marriage would be the fix for my boring life. This attitude caused me to deny the need for responsibility and action in other areas of my life. If marriage was the fix, then something and someone else would have all the responsibility for change.

I was in for a sad awakening. I had very unrealistic expectations about marriage. I originally thought that a good marriage only required both parties to be saved, love the

LORD, and love each other. It takes more, a whole lot more. I quickly grew to understand that not all love or commitment is equal, and without a conversation, you can be married to a believer and still be unequally yoked.

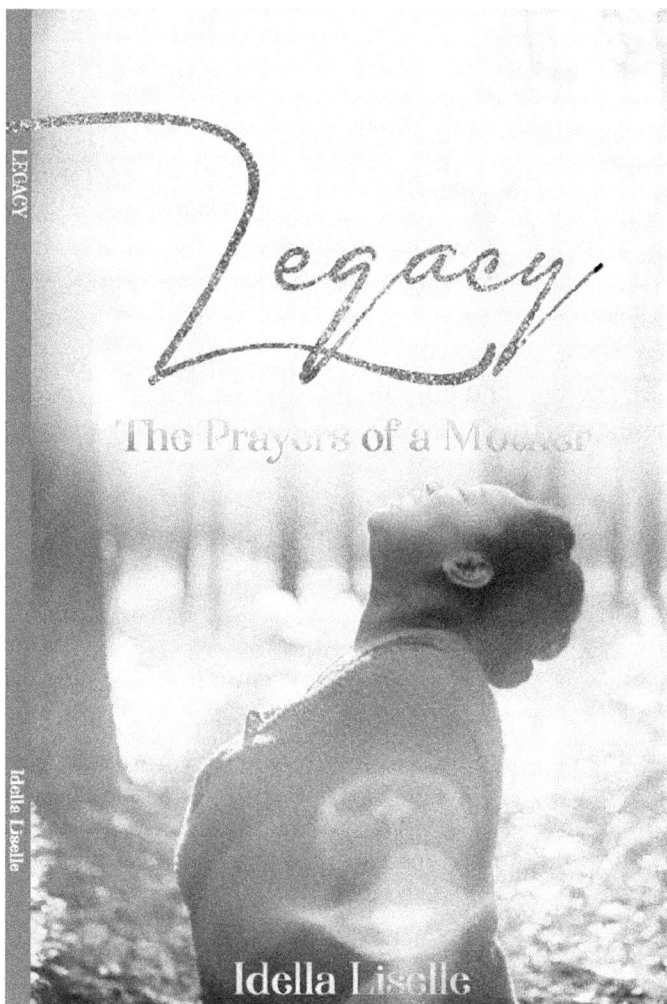

BOOK EXCERPT
LEGACY:
The Prayers of a Mother

I speak the character of CHRIST over my children and myself. Father, I thank You because JESUS CHRIST is our model, we will do greater works. I cancel any and all negative self-image problems. I thank You that neither I nor my children will struggle with acceptance of their beauty now or in the future. I thank You that whatever area that is being attacked by the enemy and highlighted negatively is being bombarded by Your love and truth. Beautify us with Your glory!

We silence the voice of the enemy and command every lie to be destroyed through Your undeniable presence in our lives. I impose the supernatural DNA of the Father through the blood of JESUS CHRIST over myself and my children. We thank You that Your divine DNA grants us everything we need for life and godliness. I plead the blood over and armor ourselves with the full armor of GOD as well as speak favor to encompass us as a shield. We receive the gift of HOLY SPIRIT, guard over our mouths to only speak the best over our lives. Thank You that my children and my words bring life and healing to the hearer. We ask that You gift us with compassion, love, kindness, mercy, grace, and victory to be in our camps. We live Your abundant life. We have the BEST LIFE.

LORD highlight, any idol that may be in our lives that is causing us to lose the guaranteed victories. Show us anything we have put on the thrones of our hearts. We thank You that as You reveal, we remove. We have the mind of CHRIST, which is in full operation in our thoughts, habits, and lives. We walk in our purpose unhindered, unimpeded and undisturbed. I command the purpose of (say the names of Your children) to come forth. I cancel confusion, indecision, and any double-mindedness to be removed from our minds regarding our purpose.

I understand that as a parent, the pursuit of my purpose is the best benefit to my children. I cancel any fears or excuses that would stop me from following after my purpose in this season. I thank You, Father, that JESUS CHRIST shepherds my children and me today, so the assignment over our lives will be complete, lacking nothing, missing nothing and no area being broken. Purpose connects us to our best lives, relationships, marriages, families, ministries, employment, business, and clients. We have favor in our present locations and even into the outer parts of the world. We receive abundant supply from all of our endeavors.

Order Your Copies Today
www.idellaliselle.com

www.ingramcontent.com/pod-product-compliance
Lightning Source LLC
Chambersburg PA
CBHW072042040426
42447CB00012BB/2973